IMAGES
of America

LOST MANITOWOC COUNTY

ON THE COVER: Fall meant silo filling time on the farm. Working together using a corn cutter and a blower in 1930 are, from left to right, Ed Ewen, Ed Hessel, and Frank Hessel on the Ed Hessel farm near Francis Creek. (Courtesy Manitowoc County Historical Society.)

IMAGES
of America

LOST MANITOWOC COUNTY

Ed Prigge

ISBN 978-1-4671-0601-6

Published by Arcadia Publishing
Charleston, South Carolina

Printed in the United States of America

Library of Congress Control Number: 2021935566

For all general information, please contact Arcadia Publishing:
Telephone 843-853-2070
Fax 843-853-0044
E-mail sales@arcadiapublishing.com
For customer service and orders:
Toll-Free 1-888-313-2665

Visit us on the Internet at www.arcadiapublishing.com

This book is dedicated to all the past, present, and future farmers of Manitowoc County.

Contents

Acknowledgments

A project like this book is never just the work of one person. This would not have been possible without the help of the Manitowoc County Historical Society, the Manitowoc Public Library, and Arcadia Publishing. Special thanks go to Amy Meyer, Meredith Gadzinski, and Phil Groll. And I could not have done this without the encouragement and support of family and friends, especially Joan Prigge, Matthew Prigge, and Angie Yamashita.

INTRODUCTION

Manitowoc County is made up of almost 600 square miles on Wisconsin's east coast. The diversity runs the gamut from its two largest cities, Manitowoc and Two Rivers, to the many small villages such as Reedsville, Valders, Mishicot, and Whitelaw and, of course, the "lost communities" like Grimms, Osman, Taus, School Hill, and Zander, just to name a few.

The rich soil, abundant trees, and natural waterways were attractive to many pioneers looking for a new place to settle down and raise their families. The years between the late 1840s and early 1850s were a busy time for immigrants to stake out their claims and brave the wild frontier. One such immigrant was Ira Clark, who in 1850 built a dual sawmill and gristmill on the Manitowoc River in the town of Cato. The village that sprung up around it would bear his name, Clarks Mills.

One of the earliest settlers in the county was Jacob Grimm. He was a boot and shoemaker living in Ohio when, in 1838, he and his wife, Margeretha, traveled to eastern Wisconsin to visit relatives. They rode through the countryside and came across a beautiful tract of land with a small stream and rolling hills. They instantly fell in love with the location and decided it was where they wanted to settle down and raise a family. As Manitowoc County continued to grow, this spot also bore his name and became Grimms. But what really put Grimms on the map is that it happens to be located on the Niagara Escarpment, which runs all the way from western New York, through upper Michigan, and down into eastern Wisconsin. It contains some of the highest-quality lime in the world. This resulted not only in a very prosperous lime business starting in Grimms but also in Rockwood and Quarry as well.

Another early settler to Manitowoc County was William Zander around 1855. The lost community of Zander bears his name. Zander is in the town of Gibson in the northern end of the county. William traveled there along with members of his family. His brother Edward had already settled here and built a log cabin. There were no roads in the area at that time, which made travel quite difficult. The family's first method of making money was by making and selling cedar shingles to a store in Mishicot. The community of Zander grew to have a blacksmith shop, general store, and a sawmill.

It was common practice to name a community after one of the early settlers, and Cooperstown was no different, being named after Allen A. Cooper. However, the first settler was Joseph Edwards, who came to the area about 1840 and built a tavern. Cooper came along just a couple of years later, and the reason it was named after him is probably because he was the first postmaster. The first school was also in Cooper's home. Father Brenner organized the first church in the community. He had already organized three other churches in the county in Manitowoc Rapids, Two Rivers, and Meeme. In later years, Cooperstown became known for its monthly cattle fair that attracted farmers from many miles away.

The village of Reedsville has a unique and interesting history. Although it was informally known as Mud Creek for a few years, it is named after Judge George Reed of Manitowoc. Reed helped to bring the railroad to Reedsville around 1860. Judge Reed died in the Newhall House fire in Milwaukee in 1883. In 1891, at a town meeting, a resolution to spend $100 to install sidewalks within the village limits was voted on and soundly defeated. The population of the growing village at that time was 510, most of them either German, Bohemian, or Irish.

The lost community of Cato is not named after a person but after Cato, New York. It was the home of Alanson Hickok, one of the earliest settlers to that area. In the early days, Cato was also known as Nettle Hill or Harris. One of its most distinctive features had always been "Cato Hill" up until the 1980s, when Highway 10 was rebuilt and the hill greatly reduced in size. There have long been rumors of an accident on that hill during Prohibition involving Al Capone. While a good story, it is likely not true. What is true is the story of one Mr. Burns who constructed the first building in the township, which he later used for printing counterfeit money. After he was caught and convicted, he spent many years in prison.

The town of Meeme was one of the four original towns of Manitowoc County. Its name comes from the Chippewa Indian language and means "pigeon." As with many towns in the second half of the nineteenth century, lumbering was an important part of the development of Meeme and its surrounding little communities such as Osman and School Hill. Hubert Simon was the first child born in the town, on February 2, 1848. Later that same year on May 9, the first marriage was performed between Nic Dittmar and a Miss Eckert.

This is just a brief history of some of the areas or rural Manitowoc County that add so much to its rich history. Some of these communities are still thriving today. Others have disappeared over the years and are just a memory. But without their contribution and the grit of those early pioneers, Manitowoc County would not be what it is today. Those communities may be lost in time, but anyone driving down the back roads can still envision them as they were a long time ago.

One

AGRICULTURE

One of the many benefits of a family farm is teaching work skills to the children. Here, two sons help their father plant corn with a four-row John Deere planter. The tractor is an Allis Chalmers, which would have been made in West Allis, Wisconsin. (Courtesy Manitowoc County Historical Society.)

In the early 20th century, all the farmers in a neighborhood would work together to harvest their grain using a threshing machine. This photograph shows a steam-powered threshing machine being used at a farm somewhere in the county. Take note of all the horse-drawn wagons used to haul the harvested grain back to the farms. (Courtesy Manitowoc County Historical Society.)

This is a typical farm scene from the early 1900s. On the far right, part of a windmill is visible. Most farms had a windmill to pump water for the barn in the days before electricity was common. (Courtesy Manitowoc County Historical Society.)

Farmers have always been able to do just about any job on the farms themselves, and building a silo is no exception. This c. 1920 photograph shows that many of these jobs were a family affair. The young man on the ground appears to be helping his father mix concrete for the silo while his younger brother looks to be having fun just being around the activity. (Courtesy Manitowoc County Historical Society.)

Many of the farms in the county are in areas that are very rocky. In the early days, the only practical use for these fields was as pasture for cattle. In addition to all the rocks seen on the surface, there are just as many or more below the surface. Before this land could be used for planting, it had to be cleared of all the rocks. (Courtesy Manitowoc County Historical Society.)

In this photograph, it looks like the threshing crew is getting ready to go out to another farm. Or perhaps they just returned from completing another farmer's crop and were getting ready for a good, hearty meal after a long day's work. (Courtesy Manitowoc County Historical Society.)

The Henry Wilhelmy farm was just south of Manitowoc in what is now the Silver Creek Park area. One of the young ladies on the bridge is holding a chicken. It was common up until the 1960s for farmers to allow their cows access to a creek for water. A barbed wire fence can be seen in the background. (Courtesy Manitowoc County Historical Society.)

Here is a photograph of an old-fashioned barn bee, or barn raising. This barn was being built at the M.T. Cooney farm in the town of Cato in 1906. Ed Ledvina was the lead carpenter on this job. When a farmer needed a new barn constructed, many of the neighbors and friends would gather to help. There was always a lead carpenter who oversaw the project. The men and older boys would work together to do the construction, and the wives and daughters would make meals to feed the crew. Many times, after it was all done, a barn dance would be held to celebrate. (Courtesy Manitowoc Public Library.)

This cheese factory in Cato was simply known as the Cato Cheese Factory. Local farmers pose in this c. 1904 photograph. At one time, there were over 100 cheese factories in Manitowoc County. Since farmers had to deliver their milk to the factory themselves each morning, they would usually choose the one closest to their farm. (Courtesy Manitowoc County Historical Society.)

This 1937 photograph of the Menges Feed Mill in Larabee shows William Menges on the right helping a local farmer load bags of feed into his horse-drawn wagon. Farmers would load their corn and oats into the wagon to bring to the mill to be ground into feed for their cows. (Courtesy Manitowoc County Historical Society.)

In the early days, farming was hard and dirty work. The hay in the fields was cut by hand, loaded onto horse-drawn wagons by hand, and then unloaded into the barns by hand. It took a special skill and experience to stack the hay on the wagon so that it could make it back to the barn without losing any along the way. (Courtesy Manitowoc County Historical Society.)

Italian immigrants are taking a break while getting the field ready for the threshing machine on the Thompson and Rienertson farm in Quarry in 1911. In the early 1900s, Manitowoc County had a large population of Italian families. They came here to work in the limestone quarries. (Courtesy Manitowoc County Historical Society.)

This photograph shows a rather unusual barn for Manitowoc County. The siding is horizontal instead of vertical. Most barns have vertical siding with spaces between the boards to allow for air circulation through the haymow. (Courtesy Manitowoc County Historical Society.)

This Rumely Oil Pull tractor is being used on a farm near Fisherville. Oil Pull tractors were built primarily in the 1920s and ran on kerosene. Rumely's first prototype tractor was built in 1909 and was called "Kerosene Annie." Rumely was the first American manufacturer of tractors to use kerosene as fuel. (Courtesy Manitowoc County Historical Society.)

This farmer is chopping hay using an Oliver 70 tractor and a Gehl chopper. The chopper is powered by its own gas engine instead of by the PTO (power take off) from the tractor. Oliver made the 70 series tractor in the 1940s. (Courtesy Manitowoc County Historical Society.)

A common sight on farms in the fall during the 1960s was picking cob corn. This unidentified farmer is using his Farmall H to harvest the corn. The corn would be stored in wire corncribs to be used all winter to grind into feed. (Courtesy Manitowoc County Historical Society.)

In 1965, the event known as Farm Progress Days, or "the World's Fair of Agriculture," was held in Manitowoc on what is now the Expo grounds. The event drew over 125,000 people during its three-day run. One of the highlights of the show was a 1,400-square-foot house built by J.J. Schmitt that was all electric. All appliances, heat, and the water heater operated on electricity. It was called "the farmhouse of the year." (Courtesy Manitowoc County Historical Society.)

The August Arneman farm was on Saxonburg Road near Mishicot. Pictured in this photograph from around the turn of the 20th century is one Mrs. Arneman, on the left, who was born, baptized, confirmed, and married in the house. Also pictured are her children George and Arthur, her sister Sidonia Lauroesch, her parents Sidonia and John Lauroesch, their hired man, and August Arneman (standing on the hay wagon). (Courtesy Manitowoc County Historical Society.)

The Brick family farm was in the town of Manitowoc Rapids at what was known as Bedells Hill, which is now the corner of Michigan Avenue and Broadway Street. Erhardt Brick is driving a team of horses pulling the grain reaper. Working the field are, from left to right, Charles, Sophie, and Ida Brick. (Courtesy Manitowoc County Historical Society.)

Because not every farmer had all the equipment needed to complete a harvest, neighboring families helped to bring in the harvest. Most everyone had at least one team of horses, and it looks like there was one farmer who had a steam engine. (Courtesy Manitowoc County Historical Society.)

The Kaltenbrun Factory was about one mile north of St. Nazianz in the early 1900s. The main product was corn-cutting equipment, which was mostly sold to local farmers. There were many of these small companies around the county that focused on making farm equipment for the area farmers. It was not unusual for these companies to make specialty equipment to meet a farmer's specific needs. (Courtesy Manitowoc County Historical Society.)

Horses were the main source of power for doing farm work around 1900. It was slow and labor-intensive for the farmers. The horses here are discing a field while another team is pulling a grain planter in the background. (Courtesy Manitowoc County Historical Society.)

A common practice for implement dealers to promote their products was to show them in use in field demonstrations. In this photograph, a farmer is trying out a John Deere two-bottom plow. This way, farmers could see different equipment in actual use under different soil and weather conditions. (Courtesy Manitowoc County Historical Society.)

This wood-stave silo was built on the Fred Sand Sr. farm on Highway 42 north of Two Rivers in 1900 for a total cost of $100. The entire silo was built in one day with the help of neighbors, family, and friends. The Sand family is seen standing in front of their new silo. (Courtesy Manitowoc County Historical Society.)

Another typical farm scene in Manitowoc County is pictured here. The rolling hills in the background may mean that this farm was in the southwest part of the county. The barbed wire fence shows that the farmer pastured his cows, as most farmers did at that time. (Courtesy Manitowoc Public Library.)

The threshing crew of Albert Maertz appears to be enjoying a cold beverage after a long, hot day of work on the Keonig farm west of Reedsville in 1915. The steam tractor is a 20-horsepower Russel. (Courtesy Manitowoc County Historical Society.)

This photograph shows a farmstead in Manitowoc County around 1960 on a gravel road. The house has a tin roof. There are two cupulas on the barn roof, and the barn was more than likely painted red, as almost all barns were at the time. The small silo indicates that this farm did not have many cows. (Courtesy Manitowoc Public Library.)

Windmills used to be a common sight on almost every farm. This one is on the David Preston farm on Preston Road near Whitelaw. Windmills were used to pump water for the cows. They always had some of the best-tasting and coldest water on hot summer days. (Courtesy Manitowoc County Historical Society.)

The farmhouse of Hiram McAllister was originally on Plank Road and was built in about 1837. It is believed to be the oldest farmhouse in Manitowoc County. McAllister farmed almost 180 acres for many years before moving back to New York in 1870. In 1998, the house was moved to Pinecrest Historical Village and now serves as the welcome center for the Manitowoc County Historical Society. (Courtesy Manitowoc County Historical Society.)

The A.W. Fischer farm was in Section No. 18 in the town of Rockland. The couple on the right are A.W. Fischer and his wife, Milia. Fischer is holding a pumpkin, so the photograph was taken in autumn. What could they be carrying on the wagon? (Courtesy Manitowoc County Historical Society.)

In 1890, Peter Kornely started the Kornely Dairy, on Highway Q just north of Manitowoc, as a cheese and butter factory. In the early 1900s, his son Charles started bottling milk in the kitchen of their house. It grew into an operation with 35 trucks delivering fresh dairy products to six counties. In 1974, the business was sold to Golden Guernsey Dairy. (Courtesy Manitowoc County Historical Society.)

Manitowoc County is home to several farms that produce maple syrup. Schools used to take field trips to some of these farms to learn how maple syrup was made. Here, Jeffrey Stock (standing) and Dennis Carter are tasting the syrup direct from the tree on the Oscar Samz farm near Mishicot. (Courtesy Manitowoc County Historical Society.)

The Oscar Samz farm near Mishicot was one of the leading producers of maple syrup in the county in the 1950s and 1960s. Four unidentified students watch as Michael Samz gathers wood to stoke the fire to keep the boiling process moving along. (Courtesy Manitowoc County Historical Society.)

Two

Businesses

Miller Implement has been a part of St. Nazianz for a long time. This photograph from 1940 shows the interior of the warehouse. The products sold over the years have changed with the times. At this time, they sold everything from kitchen ranges to manure spreaders to lawn mowers. (Courtesy Manitowoc County Historical Society.)

Pictured in 1946 is Orville Valleskey, owner of the Standard Oil gas station in Collins. The Standard Oil station was originally built by his uncle Martin Valleskey in 1930. Orville operated the station when he returned home from World War II until 1950, when he purchased a larger station in Valders. (Courtesy Manitowoc County Historical Society.)

In 1905, the quarry in Grimms was operating at full strength. Most of the buildings in this photograph were considered "company" buildings, meaning they were part of the quarry operation. Around this time, the population of Grimms was 250. (Courtesy Manitowoc County Historical Society.)

The Western Lime & Cement Co.

PIECE WORK

No. .... Date .... 192....

Name ....

....	Hours Labor	........per hour	....	....
....	Cars Lime Stone	........per car	....	
....	Cars Chips	........per car	....	....
....	Cars Crushed Stone	........per car	....	....
....	Loads Bldg. Stone	........per load	....	....
....	....	per load	....	....
....	....		....	....
	Total Earnings			

Form 48 5M-9-28 2014.103b

This is a 1920s work form for the Western Lime & Cement Company, which owned the quarry in Grimms in the early 1900s. Laborers would keep track of how much work they did each day, and their pay was based on a piece rate, meaning the more work they did, the more they would earn. (Courtesy Manitowoc County Historical Society.)

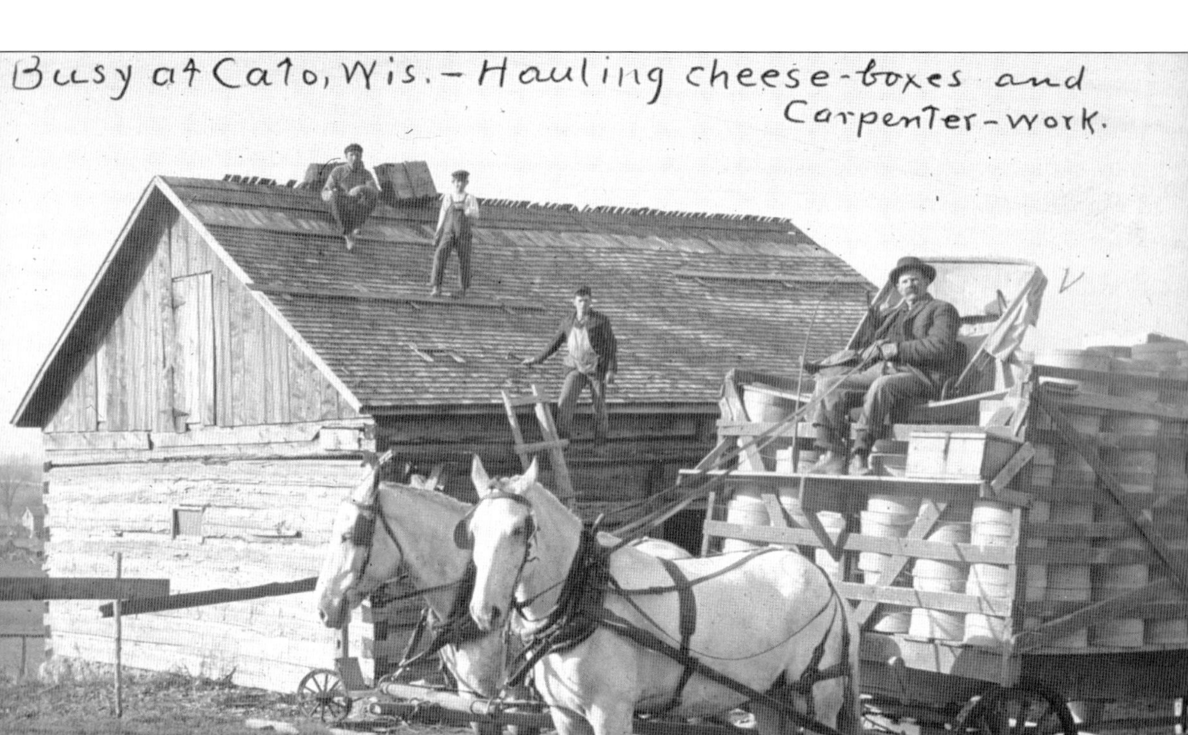

This photograph, taken near Cato, shows two different activities taking place. In the background, there is a crew putting cedar shake shingles on a barn roof. The man in the wagon is hauling a load of cheese boxes to a local cheese factory. It is possible that the father is driving the wagon and his sons are working on the roof. (Courtesy Manitowoc Public Library.)

In 1911, the Gartzke Brothers Brewing Company operated the brewery in Hika. Replacing the original building that was destroyed by fire in the 1880s, this facility was built in 1890; however, it was torn down in 1914, and the bricks were used to build the Mikadow Theatre in Manitowoc. (Courtesy Manitowoc County Historical Society.)

This photograph shows Orville Vallesky inside his "office" at his Standard Oil station in Valders in 1950. He won numerous awards from Standard Oil for how clean he kept his station. The small box on top of the cash register is for Doublemint gum. (Courtesy Manitowoc County Historical Society.)

Orville Vallesky opened his Standard Oil station on Calumet Avenue in Valders on October 27, 1950. His station offered full service, as all stations did at that time. Full service meant filling the tank, washing the windows, and checking the oil. The building is still there and now houses Dave Mahlik State Farm Insurance. (Courtesy Manitowoc County Historical Society.)

Work inside the lime kilns in Grimms was hot, hard, and dirty. This photograph from about 1900 shows some of the laborers. Many of the workers came to Manitowoc County from Italy to work in the quarry. At that time, many of the residents of Grimms were Italian. The man at far left is Peter Gosz. (Courtesy Manitowoc County Historical Society.)

Facing east from on top of the hill in Grimms, this photograph shows firewood for Western Lime Company's kilns, which cooked raw limestone into usable lime. Farmers would make extra money selling firewood to the quarry. At its peak in the early 1900s, the Western Lime Company produced some of the world's finest lime from its quarry in Grimms. The quarry ceased operations in 1928. (Courtesy Manitowoc County Historical Society.)

Pictured here is the opening to an oven in the lime kilns in Grimms. There were about 10 or 12 of these in the kilns. Firewood was placed inside to create intense heat to break the raw limestone down into usable lime, which was sold worldwide. This was very dangerous and hot work, and it was not unusual for the fires to get out of control. (Courtesy Manitowoc County Historical Society.)

This photograph from about 1920 shows Frank Stastny standing behind the bar at the Stastny Hotel and Bar in Francis Creek. At the time, Francis Creek had a population of almost 200 and was the largest community in the town of Kossuth. The poster behind Stastny mentions a grand ball that was being held at the opera house in Branch. (Courtesy Manitowoc County Historical Society.)

William Menges and his wife, Nora, owned the Clover farm store in Larrabee in the 1950s. From left to right are William, Nora, Nora's sister Esther, and her husband, Dwight Holsapple. (Courtesy Manitowoc County Historical Society.)

The Charles Lodel meat market and general store was in Tisch Mills. In the early 1900s, almost all small communities in the county had their own stores and meat markets. In many cases, the store owners and their families lived above the store. (Courtesy Manitowoc County Historical Society.)

Built by Joe Stangel, the County Line House was in Tisch Mills. Pictured around 1910, it also housed the first post office in Tisch Mills. Much later, the Tisch Mills State Bank would be built on this site. The occasion for this formal group photograph was likely a wedding or anniversary party. (Courtesy Manitowoc County Historical Society.)

In 1911, William F. Christel of Valders owned a hardware store and sold farm equipment. Next to his hardware store, he opened one of the first Ford dealerships in the state of Wisconsin. Over the years, the Christel family would own and operate several different types of businesses in the village. (Courtesy Manitowoc County Historical Society.)

The Lakeland Egg Cooperative operated in Valders from 1949 to 1976. It expanded its operations in 1953, and again in 1964. It ceased operations in 1976 and sold the building. Bernadine Ryan is seen here in 1953 sorting eggs. (Courtesy Manitowoc County Historical Society.)

Wenzel Sykora learned the harness-making trade at Kumbalek's Harness Shop in Kewaunee when he was 15 years old. He eventually moved to Tisch Mills to open his own shop in 1886. His son Edwin took over the business and ran it until 1956, when he passed away at the age of 72. The original building is still in Tisch Mills. (Courtesy Manitowoc County Historical Society.)

Many of the small communities had feed mills like Tisch Mill's Milling Company to provide farmers all their seed-and-feed needs. In this photograph from the late 1950s, a local farmer is loading his truck with ground feed to take back to his farm. Note the King Midas Flour sign on the building. (Courtesy Manitowoc County Historical Society.)

Welcoming thirsty people into this country tavern is likely the proprietor. Country bars were more than just a place to wet one's whistle. They also were the place to catch up on all the local gossip and meet with friends. Note the sign for Fox Head 400 beer. It was thought that Fox Head was owned by the mob. (Courtesy Manitowoc Public Library.)

Three

COMMUNITIES

Most communities had their own general stores. This c. 1908 photograph shows the Pritzl general store in Clarks Mills. Originally built in the 1870s, it had numerous owners over the years. Mike and Catherina Pritzl ran the store prior to 1910, and William and Rose Klann owned it between 1910 and 1926. It was moved to Pinecrest Historical Village in 1988. (Courtesy Manitowoc County Historical Society.)

John Nespar poses with his horse Reindeer in front of the Albert Svacina hotel and saloon in Grimms in 1905. Note the two Rahr's Beer signs on the building. Early on, the bar was owned by William, Reinhardt, and Max Rahr. The Rahr family owned saloons throughout the county in order to have places to sell their beer. (Courtesy Manitowoc County Historical Society.)

The village of Rockwood gets its name from the two lime companies that used to be there, Rockwell and Allwood. Gosz's Bar is on the left just above the road, and the old Rockwood School is the two-story brick building on the right. (Courtesy Manitowoc County Historical Society.)

Manitowoc Rapids was the first county seat for Manitowoc County and home of its first courthouse and jail. Joseph Conroe opened the first post office there in 1836. This is a view from the early 1900s looking north toward the hill on what is now Rapids Road. The bridge has since been replaced twice. (Courtesy Manitowoc County Historical Society.)

Named after a community in New York, the lost community of Cato was once known as Nettle Hill. The tall building in the background is the grain elevator. The building stills stands but is no longer operative. (Courtesy Manitowoc County Historical Society.)

In 1899, Joseph Holly Sr. and Charles Hacker built a dual sawmill and gristmill in Shoto. In 1908, Holly became the sole owner when Hacker moved to Manitowoc. The mill was destroyed by fire in 1949. The fire was so large that it could be seen 30 miles away. Three local fire departments fought the fire for over six hours, but the structure was a total loss. (Courtesy Manitowoc County Historical Society.)

The village of Clarks Mills has had a few interesting stories over the years, but maybe the most fascinating story is from 1966 when an alligator was said to have been spotted in the river. It drew the attention of statewide media and alligator hunters. The sightings lasted over three months, but the alligator was never found. (Courtesy Manitowoc County Historical Society.)

The Collins Volunteer Fire Department was formed in 1904. This is the first fire engine house, which was built in 1905. In 1908, the department purchased a buggy from August Born for $10 and converted it into a hook-and-ladder wagon. The hook and ladders were made by Henry Schnell for $185. (Courtesy Manitowoc County Historical Society.)

During the early years of Manitowoc County, there were many small churches. This former Presbyterian church was just south of Cato on Highway J. It served its congregation for many years before meeting the same fate of many other small churches and closed because of declining membership. It was razed through a controlled burn in 1978. (Courtesy Manitowoc County Historical Society.)

The once bustling lime kilns in Grimms sat dormant for about 60 years before this structure was demolished in the mid-1980s. The railroad tracks that run along the top of the kilns are still visible. In its last years, this building was used by a local farmer for storing hay. (Courtesy Manitowoc County Historical Society.)

When the quarry was operating at full capacity in the early 1920s, the train seen here on top of the kilns would haul railcars full of limestone from the quarry to dump into the kilns, which heated and turned it into lime that was shipped all over the United States. (Courtesy Manitowoc County Historical Society.)

Another one of Manitowoc County's lost communities is Fisherville, which was home to the Fisherville Tavern and Dance Hall. The man on the wagon at left is Henry Hagenow. John Fisher, the owner of the establishment, is second from the left on the steps. The other people are all members of the Chaloupka and Kronforst families. Lillian Hagenow's dog Pepper runs in front. (Courtesy Manitowoc County Historical Society.)

A group of people have gathered in front of a dance hall and saloon in this c. 1910 photograph from Kellnersville. It would appear by their dress that they might have been attending a wedding or some other formal event. (Courtesy Manitowoc County Historical Society.)

Dr. J.B. Rick was the local doctor in Larrabee. His house was adjacent to his office. From left to right are Dr. Rick, Lillie Rick, and their children Elsie and Ruth. The dog's name is not known. (Courtesy Manitowoc County Historical Society.)

The community of Maple Grove was founded by Irish settlers in the 1850s. Tom Morrissey was one of the first settlers when he started a small store and saloon. St. Patrick's Church is shown here on the left. In its heyday in the early 1900s, Maple Grove had three stores, four saloons, two hotels, a dance hall, an ice cream parlor, a church, a school, and a funeral home. (Courtesy Manitowoc County Historical Society.)

The Maribel Caves Hotel was built in 1900 from limestone native to the area. It has an extraordinarily rich and colorful history. In its early years, it could host over 200 guests a day and had 42 guest rooms. The history of the property, which includes gangster stories, deserves a book of its own. (Courtesy Manitowoc County Historical Society.)

The Badger State Hotel, sometimes known as the Badger State House, was on the corner of East Main and Jackson Streets in Mishicot. The building was very ornate and had tin ceilings. It is still standing today. This photograph was taken around 1880. (Courtesy Manitowoc County Historical Society.)

The Poll House in the town of Meeme was built in 1900 by Joseph Schwartz and Edmund Kolb. It provided a place for residents to vote for over 80 years. Here, voters made their choices using paper ballots and dropping them in a box. The Poll House is now part of Pinecrest Historical Village. (Courtesy Manitowoc County Historical Society.)

The lost community of School Hill was home to Pritzl's Community Garage around 1920. Most small-town gas stations only had one gas pump, but Pritzl's had three and also offered car repair. The building still stands today. (Courtesy Manitowoc County Historical Society.)

In 1961, Branch was the scene of a major train derailment. A total of 15 cars and the engine ran off the tracks when a wheel broke on one of the boxcars. The train was carrying paper products from Kaukauna to Manitowoc. No one was injured. In 1910, there was another derailment in almost the exact same spot. In that accident, three cars tipped over. Two of the cars were carrying lime from the quarry in Grimms. (Courtesy Manitowoc County Historical Society.)

This c. 1909 photograph is looking west on Washington Street in Valders. The building partially visible on the left was the Valders Hotel and post office. Later, this would become the Willows Supper Club. Also on the left is Aubol Hardware and the Rabe blacksmith shop and livery stable. Note the sign for the Ringling Bros. Circus. (Courtesy Manitowoc County Historical Society.)

Here is another Washington Street scene from Valders, from 1914. The large building on the right was a grocery store run by Joe Sipper; later, it would become the home of the *Valders Journal*. Note all the postings for the county fair and signs for Old Painter tobacco. (Courtesy Manitowoc County Historical Society.)

Downtown Mishicot has seen many floods over the years. This 1980 flood took place in the spring. Pictured are the Mishicot Laundromat, Kronforst Electric, and Krajnik Chevrolet. (Courtesy Manitowoc County Historical Society.)

Zander is a lost community in the northern end of Manitowoc County. It was built up around the intersection of what is now Highway Q and Zander Road. Only a few houses now remain in this community that was named for John Zander, one of its first settlers. It was once home to a school, general store, and a saloon. (Courtesy Manitowoc County Historical Society.)

The Salvatorian Seminary in St. Nazianz opened in 1909 with a class of 14 young men studying for the priesthood. It served in that capacity until 1968, when the entire complex became the home of John F. Kennedy Preparatory, still under the operation of the Salvatorians. The first year, the enrollment was limited to male students, with females enrolling in the second year of operation. (Courtesy Manitowoc County Historical Society.)

This drawing from 1854 shows an early St. Nazianz. The large building at top right is St. Gregory School. Rev. Ambrose Oschwald founded the village of St. Nazianz. (Courtesy Manitowoc County Historical Society.)

The now lost community of Quarry was once highly active with a limestone quarry and various businesses. Its train depot was busy with trains not only carrying lime from the quarry but also delivering passengers, mail, and goods twice a day. The depot was moved to Amhurst Junction in 1964. (Courtesy Manitowoc County Historical Society.)

This photograph shows the St. James Evangelical Lutheran Church in Newtonburg. This church was built in 1868 and replaced the original log cabin church that was built in 1857. (Courtesy Manitowoc Public Library.)

Four

SCHOOLS

The entire student body of the Rockwood school and their teacher pose for the 1954 class picture. The Rockwood School has some interesting footnotes in its history. In 1871, it was resolved that the school would be closed on Sundays, and all religious meetings would be prohibited from taking place in the school. In 1872, it was ordered that the teacher had to be able to teach German two days a week and English three days a week. (Courtesy Manitowoc County Historical Society.)

Students at the Newtonburg School are practicing their dance moves. It looks like this activity might have been part of a play the school put on based on the costumes the students are wearing. The boys do not exactly look thrilled. (Courtesy Manitowoc County Historical Society.)

This 1898 class photograph is from the Newton School. This would have been considered a large class for that era. The slates that the children are holding show that the school was divided into four classes, A, B, C, and D. The teachers were Ida Schneider and Karl Zander. Male teachers were usually paid more than female teachers at that time. Zander may have made $40 for the school term, and Schneider may have made about $30. (Courtesy Manitowoc Public Library.)

Students, community members, and construction workers pose during the building of the new Newtonburg School in 1936. The building and all equipment cost $15,500 and was considered one of the most modern schools in the state. It had a full basement, indoor bathrooms, and a central heating and ventilation system. (Courtesy Manitowoc County Historical Society.)

Teacher Harold Drumm is seen here posing with his students for their 1934 class photograph. The Center School was also known as the Nenning School because the Nenning family lived across the road. The name was officially changed to Center School in 1918 because it was located on Highway 141 halfway between Manitowoc and Sheboygan. (Courtesy Manitowoc County Historical Society.)

This 1954 class photograph from the Grimms School shows all the students. At this time, the school had grades one through eight. Elmer Uhleg taught at the school for only a few years. The author's brother Gary is in the second row at far left, sister Joyce is standing directly behind the teacher, and sister Jane is in the first row on the far right. All six Prigge children attended this school. (Courtesy Manitowoc County Historical Society.)

This was the third building to be used as a school in Grimms. It was built in 1869 for a cost of $500. At its peak in the 1920s, there were about 70 students in the two classrooms. In 1928, twelve-year-old Esther Bebow, a sixth grader at the school, finished second in the state spelling bee. The school operated until 1963, when it closed, and the students transferred to Reedsville. At the time, there were only 10 students in grades one through six, and the school still did not have running water or indoor bathrooms. (Courtesy Manitowoc County Historical Society.)

This is another Herman Benke school class picture in an outdoor setting. This is Cooperstown District No. 3 School, later known as the Hickory Grove School. This photograph is of the 1898 class, with teacher Anna Bradley. The school year was divided into a winter term and a summer term. The winter term usually had a male teacher, and the summer term had a female teacher, as many of the male teachers were also farmers who had to work their farms during the summer. (Courtesy Manitowoc Public Library.)

Herman Benke paid tribute to the rich German heritage of the county by captioning this school photograph in German. It reads, "The Evangelical Lutheran St. Johns local community school at Maribel." It appears the writing on the blackboard may also be in German. (Courtesy Manitowoc Public Library.)

Charles Meisnest taught at the school in Rockwood in 1898 and 1899. The school building at that time was brand new and was used until 1924, when increasing enrollment necessitated a larger school because of the increasing population in the Rockwood area. (Courtesy Manitowoc Public Library.)

A favorite day in grade school was when the class would take a field trip. These students are at the Oscar Samz farm near Mishicot to learn how maple syrup is made. From left to right are Ann Labinski, John Grosshuesch, Mike Mella, Danny Braley, Daniel Flaim, Dennis Hubbert, and Mike Tellefson. Oscar Samz is on the right. (Courtesy Manitowoc County Historical Society.)

In the early days of the county, there would often be what were called joint school districts. These would be in an area where more than one township would join to have a school. This photograph from 1899 shows the Rockland, Eaton, and Cato school districts. Its official name was the Fair View School because it had a "fair view" of the surrounding farms and river. However, many people referred to it as the Quarry School because of its proximity to Quarry. (Courtesy Manitowoc Public Library.)

The slate on the right reads, "The groves were God's first temples." This same slate is seen in many of Herman Benke's class photographs from the late 1800s. This class is from Mishicot School District No. 4 in 1899. The teacher was John Schambeau. Note the dog and an alarm clock in the foreground. This school was originally known as the French Settlement School and then was named LaSalle School. (Courtesy Manitowoc Public Library.)

The Branch School was just south of Branch, and it appears from this late 1890s photograph that it offered some classes that focused on agriculture. As was typical in that era, the boys sat on one side of the room and the girls on the other. The teacher seems to be explaining the different types of corn that can be grown in the area. (Courtesy Manitowoc Public Library.)

In this 1899 photograph, the slate reads, "Go forth into the woods and listen to nature's teachings." The teacher for Gibson District School was Peter Federspiel. The school was also called the Holmes School after poet Oliver Wendell Holmes. because so many of the students liked his poetry. (Courtesy Manitowoc Public Library.)

The Kossuth District No. 1 School was just north of Francis Creek and was named the Francis Creek School. The brick schoolhouse, shown here in 1912, was built in 1891. It did not have a basement because the amount of rocks in the area made that difficult. Electric lights were installed in 1935. The playground equipment consisted of swings and a slide. In 1912, it was one of the larger schools in the county with an enrollment of about 60. (Courtesy Manitowoc County Historical Society.)

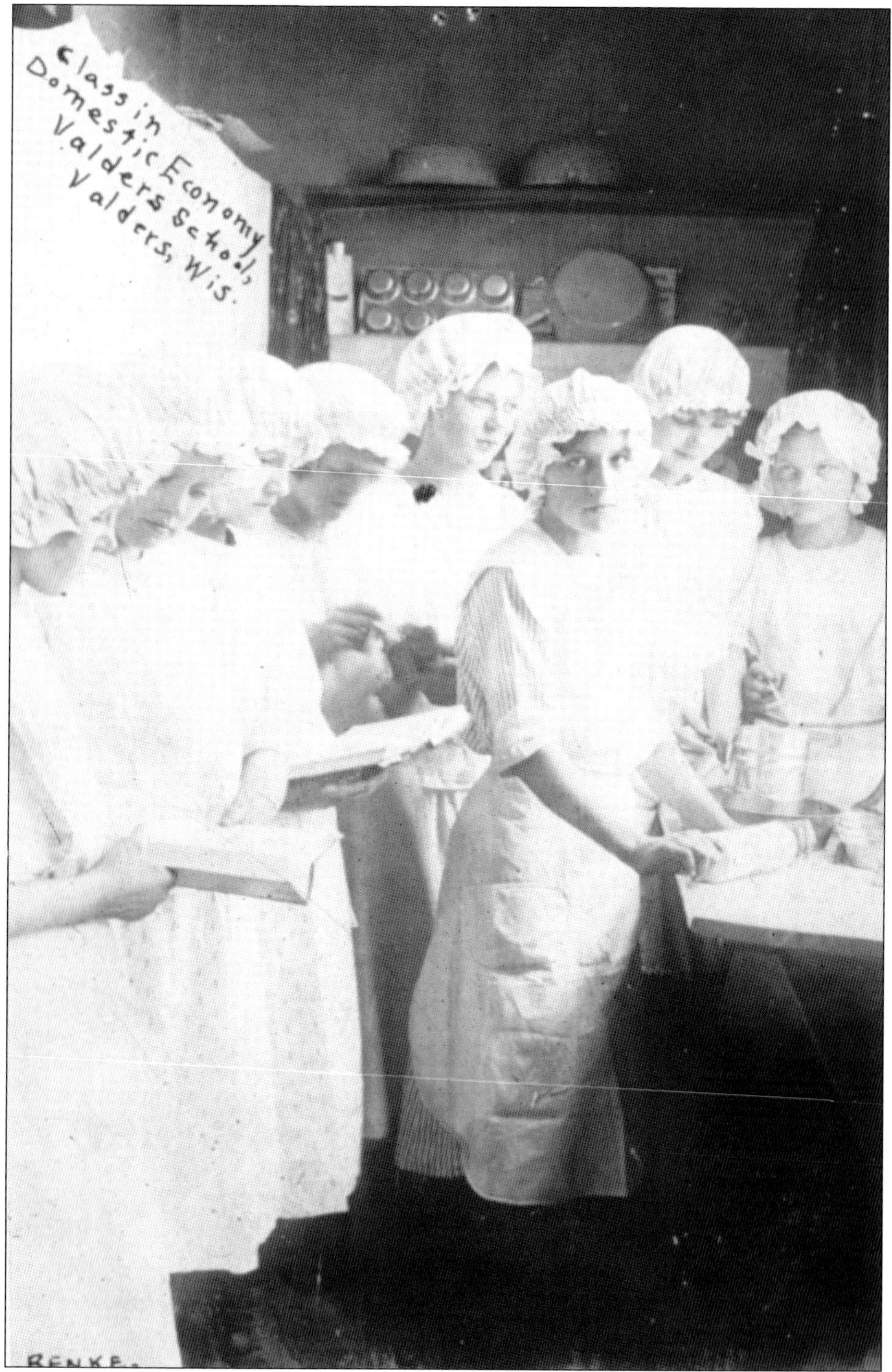

This photograph of an early 1900s domestic economy class from Valders High School shows the young ladies getting ready to bake. These classes were for girls only in those days. Later, the class would be called home economics. Note the muffin tin, cast-iron frying pan, and cheese grater on the shelves in the back. (Courtesy Manitowoc Public Library.)

At this unnamed school, students are lining up to get a hot lunch, which was quite unusual. It is possible the teacher brought in some homemade soup to feed the students on a cold winter day. At that time, students would either bring a bag lunch to school or walk home for lunch if they lived nearby. The teacher also had to bring a bag lunch. (Courtesy Manitowoc County Historical Society.)

The Branch School is pictured in 1900. All the students in this photograph probably did not attend the school at the same time. There was usually a summer term and a winter term so that farm families had their boys home during the summer to help with the farm work. (Courtesy Manitowoc County Historical Society.)

The Brockville School was near Francis Creek in a now lost area originally called Cinder Dump. The school in this 1908 photograph was the original school, built in 1903. Peter Hronek did the masonry work, and Joe Stransky was the carpenter. The total construction cost was $2,300. The teacher in the photograph is Mary Conway. (Courtesy Manitowoc County Historical Society.)

The school in Cato Joint District No. 9 was called the Lowell School, named after poet James R. Lowell. It was about a mile and a half south of Grimms. At times, it was also known as the South Grimms School or the Denk School because it was across the road from the James Denk farm. This brick structure was built in 1924. (Courtesy Manitowoc County Historical Society.)

All nine students who attended Lowell School in 1956 are pictured here with their teacher, Beatrice Lang. The school closed the following year. The average attendance in the school's early years was between 35 and 40 pupils, but as more parochial schools came to the area, attendance declined every year. (Courtesy Manitowoc County Historical Society.)

These four students from the Center School near Centerville are in science class in 1952. The two standing are reading a book about birds, and the two on the floor are looking at butterflies and a bird's nest. Their teacher was Margaret Gruber. (Courtesy Manitowoc County Historical Society.)

The school called Franklin District No. 13 was in Taus and was named after Benjamin Franklin. In this 1899 photograph, the teacher was Hannah Lorrigan. Note the numerous stone arrow points, spears, and hatchets uncovered by farmers working the land in the vicinity of this school over the years. This indicates that this was probably a prime hunting spot for Native Americans. (Courtesy Manitowoc County Historical Society.)

One of the highlights of the year for all rural schools was the Christmas program. This was the program in 1948 for Shadyside School. The teacher was Mrs. Walter Hoyer. The students are, in unknown order, Ordella Fisher, Roman Gaedtke, Delmar Thomas, Dianne Erdman, John Erdman, Reinhardt Gaedtke, John Krueger, Donald Erdman, Elaine Erdman, Edward Kretsch, Edward Vetting, David Puls, Harlan Gaedtke, Judith Waack, Dick Erdman, Mary Brunner, Tom Brunner, Herman Gaedtke, and Ruth Ann Engelbrecht. (Courtesy Manitowoc County Historical Society.)

In 1914, Shadyside School added an enclosed front entrance, which allowed students to store their coats and boots inside. This photograph shows, from left to right, William Fisher, teacher Edna Mittnacht, Walter Vetting, and Alex Kaufman. (Courtesy Manitowoc County Historical Society.)

The Shadyside School was on Highway 151 about five miles west of Manitowoc and served School District No. 1 for the town of Manitowoc Rapids. It was built in 1872 after fire destroyed the original log cabin school in 1871. It was also called the Irish School and the Trainor School. The name was changed to Shadyside because of the box elder trees around the school. The school closed in 1956, and in 1976, the building was moved to Pinecrest Historical Village for a cost of $5,645. (Courtesy Manitowoc County Historical Society.)

Students and teachers look on as John Sowkowski of the telephone company shows them how he climbs a pole in 1953 at the Marquette School in Maple Grove. Almost all rural schools had telephone service by this time. Those that did not needed to rely on a neighbor if a phone was needed. (Courtesy Manitowoc County Historical Society.)

There is not a lot of recorded history of the harmonica band from the White Trail School in Newton. But from this 1935 photograph, it appears that quite a bit of effort went into their work. They probably played at school events and gatherings in the community. Imagine trying to teach 21 youngsters how to play the harmonica! (Courtesy Manitowoc County Historical Society.)

The Taylor School in the town of Meeme was known as a singing and music school because it was a leader in the county in teaching music. This photograph from 1937 shows the students with a variety of instruments. The music teachers were Dorothy Mueller, Theodore Wimmler, and Phyliss Schmidt. (Courtesy Manitowoc County Historical Society.)

The Maple Corner School was in the town of Schleswig near Millhome. It was also referred to as the Millhome School. The school building seen here was built in 1888 by Herman Dexheimer for $715. In the 1890s, the school had almost 60 students enrolled, but by 1948, enrollment was down to 26. (Courtesy Manitowoc County Historical Society.)

The Twin River School was in the town of Cooperstown near the Twin River. It was known by locals as the Radue School because it was on the William Radue farm. Note the outhouses in this 1950 photograph. It can be assumed that the school also did not have running water, which was quite common for rural schools at that time. There was always a boys' outhouse and a girls' outhouse. In some cases, there was a third outhouse just for the teacher. (Courtesy Manitowoc County Historical Society.)

This school was for Cato Joint School District No. 3 and was on Highway J on top of the hill north of Valders. Some of the locals called it the Aubol School, possibly because of the Ole Aubol family who lived in the area. It was built in 1906 for $2,500. The second floor was not finished until 1910 because it initially only had one teacher and not enough students to fill both floors. (Courtesy Manitowoc County Historical Society.)

Schoolchildren are dancing around a traditional maypole at the county fairgrounds. It looks like this may have been part of a bigger event, possibly a May Day celebration involving many of the rural grade schools. (Courtesy Manitowoc Public Library.)

In this c. 1920 photograph, a graduating class of St. Mary's school, run by Holy Family Convent of Manitowoc in Reedsville, is pictured. At far left is Sister Basilia, and Sister Aquilina is at far right. The family names of some of the students are Svatek, Bergman, and Hickey. (Courtesy Manitowoc Public Library.)

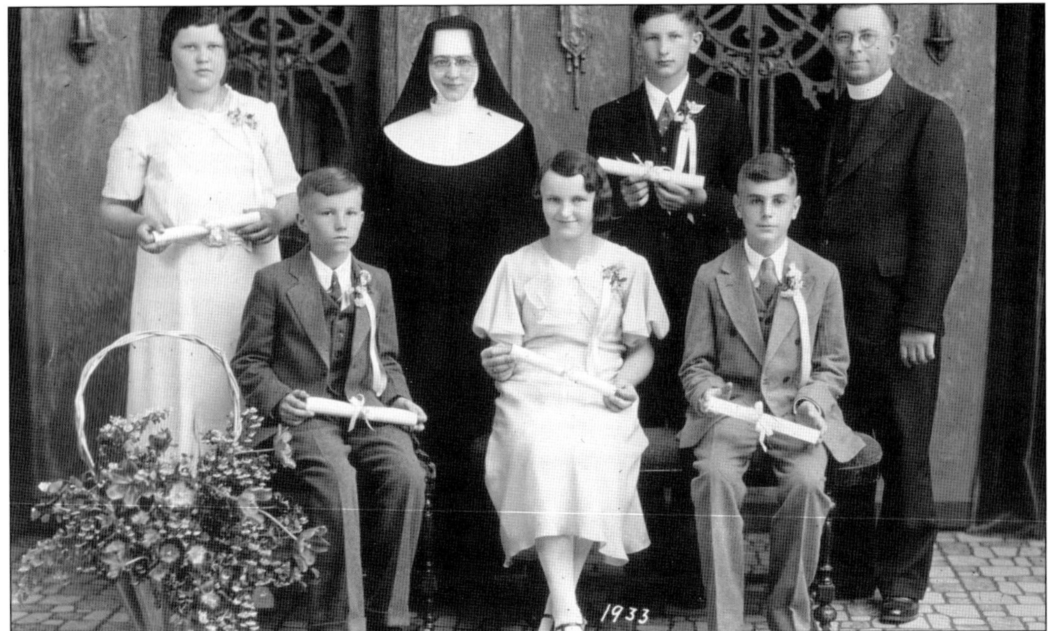

St. Mary's Catholic Church and grade school was a fixture in Reedsville for many years. These five students were the confirmation class of 1933. From left to righ are (first row) Joseph Shimek, Julia Burich, and Norbert Wojta; (second row) Ruth Schuh, unidentified, Edward Kubale, and unidentified. (Courtesy Manitowoc Public Library.)

In 1940, thirty-one students graduated from Valders High School. They are shown here along with the school principal, C.E. Bray, and their class advisor, Helen Lauderdale. Bray was named principal of the school in 1924 and served in that position for 37 years. The first class graduated in 1924. (Courtesy Manitowoc County Historical Society.)

This 1910 photograph is of the first graduating class of St. Wendal's School in Cleveland. Sisters Pacifica Isselman (far left) and Jeanette Sunville (second from left) were from Holy Family Convent in Manitowoc. Sister Jeanette was also the principal and taught seventh and eighth grades at the school. (Courtesy Manitowoc Public Library.)

Five

Rural Life

A group of men enjoy a few cold brews at the bar in Maple Grove in 1892. Seated at the table are, from left to right, J.P. Watt, Dan Lorrigan, and Thomas Watt Sr. Standing in the back at the left side of the bar is the beer wagon driver. The bartender is Mike Hennesey, and in front of the bar are Fred Siegler Jr. and Fred Seigler Sr. The two children standing on top of the bar are Cora (left) and Eddie Watt. (Courtesy Manitowoc County Historical Society.)

Manitowoc County has numerous lakes that provide many types of recreation. This photograph shows Herman Benke, his sister Ida, and their father, Carl, enjoying a day of fishing on Bullhead Lake in the western part of the county. Based on how Herman and Ida are dressed, one would guess that Carl did most of the catching. (Courtesy Manitowoc Public Library.)

This photograph could be captioned, "The photographer getting ready to take a photo." It shows Herman Benke crossing a log to get into a swampy area to take another photograph of the natural beauty of Manitowoc County. Benke took thousands of photographs throughout the county. (Courtesy Manitowoc Public Library.)

A road crew takes a break from what looks to be working a stone crusher. In the early days, there were very few paved roads in the county. Eventually, the dirt roads were upgraded to gravel, and finally paved. (Courtesy Manitowoc Public Library.)

On August 8, 1909, a monument was dedicated to Chief Mexico in Manitowoc Rapids on what is now Broadway Street. Chief Mexico was instrumental in negotiating peace between the Native Americans and the early settlers of Manitowoc County. (Courtesy Manitowoc Public Library.)

This pioneer log house was in the town of Cooperstown in the Devils River area. When the early settlers moved to Manitowoc County in the late 1800s, they often would buy a 40-acre parcel of land and use the trees to build their first home. Very few are still standing today. (Courtesy Manitowoc County Historical Society.)

English Lake has always been a popular spot in Manitowoc County. For many years, people have come here to swim, boat, fish, and just get away from the city. In the early 1900s, some people who lived in Manitowoc had small vacation cottages on the lake. Very few people lived on the lake full-time at that time. (Courtesy Manitowoc Public Library.)

The Manitowoc River at Lower Cato Falls has always been a popular fishing spot. These two men in 1890 appear to be enjoying the beautiful weather and possibly hoping the fish do not bite and ruin their relaxing day. (Courtesy Manitowoc Public Library.)

Early travel in Manitowoc County was an adventure. Before any roads were paved, they were simply dirt. The condition of the roads would mostly dictate when and where one went. Here, three men are dressed up and going for a ride. They might have been on their way to church, or perhaps to an evening of card playing at their favorite local saloon. (Courtesy Manitowoc Public Library.)

For a time during the 1940s, Svacina's Bar in Grimms was known as the Lime City Tavern, paying homage to the village's rich history. Posing in front of the bar are Carol Stefl (left) and Regina Svacina. Regina and her husband, Ray, were longtime owners of the establishment. (Courtesy Manitowoc County Historical Society.)

David Gauthier (seated at upper right wearing a white shirt) was a band instructor, and each year, he would hold a recital with his guitar and accordion students in Kellnersville. In 1937, the recital was held at Kubsch's Hall in downtown Kellnersville. (Courtesy Manitowoc County Historical Society.)

These four men were rehearsing for a play at the Meeme House Inn in 1915. From left to right are Joe Schwartz (owner), Frank Herr, Joe Wasmer, and Frank Fischer. The Meeme House Inn hosted a variety of plays and shows in the early 1900s. It was purchased by The Manitowoc County Historical Society and relocated to Pinecrest Historical Village in 2018. (Courtesy Manitowoc County Historical Society.)

Looking very dapper in his vest and bowler hat is Peter DeGroot, the owner of the Meeme House Inn from 1906 to 1909. He sold the Meeme House to Joseph Schwartz in 1909, and it stayed in his family until it closed. (Courtesy Manitowoc County Historical Society.)

Adolph Chaloupka, owner of the cheese factory in Larabee, stands on the street with his children. The large building in the background is the Kronforst Tavern. The smaller building on the left is a shed owned by the township. The sign advertises a circus that would be in the area on May 20. (Courtesy Manitowoc County Historical Society.)

The Newton State Bank celebrated its silver jubilee in 1946. Shown here from left to right are bank president Edward Rhode, vice president William Belitz, Otto Schmitz, Erwin Bruckchen, Frank O'Neil, Herman Eberhardt, and Jacob Zych. (Courtesy Manitowoc County Historical Society.)

Standing at the entrance to the Maribel Caves are, from left to right, Ernst Pleuss, Ida Giese, Bertha Giese, Marie Giese, and John Glander. Glander was a highly successful photographer in Manitowoc. He married Marie Giese in 1910. (Courtesy Manitowoc County Historical Society.)

The Edward Fritzi home was built in 1866. In 1875, the house was purchased by Fritzi's neighbor Christian Carstens. It remained in the Carstens family for about 100 years until 1978, when it was donated to the Manitowoc County Historical Society and moved to Pinecrest Historical Village, where it became the village saloon after renovations. (Courtesy Manitowoc County Historical Society.)

Many of the rural communities had a basketball team, and Osman was no exception. The Osman Scrubs of the Osman Athletic Association consisted of, from left to right, (first row) James Driscoll, Ray O'Neil, and James Conway; (second row) Gary O'Neil, Steve Egan, and August Lenz. (Courtesy Manitowoc County Historical Society.)

One of the more popular hangouts in Quarry in the early 1900s was the Aeroplane Inn, a combination saloon, hotel, and dance hall. The man at far left is Rudy Moderhock, owner of the establishment. He is taking a break to play cards with friends. His rubber sleeves were used for protection while carrying blocks of ice. (Courtesy Manitowoc County Historical Society.)

In the late 1800s and early 1900s, bands and orchestras were extremely popular forms of entertainment. They would play at dance halls and opera houses throughout the county. Sometimes, they would give free concerts in the park on Sunday afternoons. This is the Ferdinand Fraenzel Orchestra in 1894. (Courtesy Manitowoc Public Library.)

This 13-man mason crew is taking a break from the construction of a shed in the town of Two Creeks. Some of the rafters for the ceiling are already in place. Many work crews like this were made up of mostly family members. (Courtesy Manitowoc County Historical Society.)

This 1945 photograph was taken in front of the Standard Oil station in Rockwood and shows Romy Gosz (right), "the Polka King," and Earl Bleser. This is now the site of the Big Apple. (Courtesy Manitowoc County Historical Society.)

Romy Gosz was known around the United States as "the Polka King." In 1941, he received national attention when he was featured in a photograph spread and story in *Life* magazine. His seven-piece orchestra toured the country playing at dances, weddings, and parties. (Courtesy Manitowoc Public Library.)

This 1906 photograph from the Reedsville area shows the mason crew of Albert Prochnow working on the stone foundation of a barn on the Burish farm. The stones were hauled from nearby fields and quarries. Building a barn foundation like this was very labor intensive. (Courtesy Manitowoc County Historical Society.)

A large wedding party is gathered outside of Kulyn's Tavern around the turn of the 20th century. It is possible the tavern was only in business for a short time, because no record of its location could be found. A six-piece brass band played at this wedding. (Courtesy Manitowoc County Historical Society.)

Five soldiers sit outside their tent while on a break from training. From left to right are E.A. Hartman, Joh Franz Jr., Emil Baensch, C.A. Groffman, and William Abel. Baensch was the captain of Company H of the 2nd Regiment of the Wisconsin National Guard from 1883 to 1888. He was also a lawyer and a judge and is credited with starting the Manitowoc County Historical Society. (Courtesy Manitowoc Public Library.)

This photograph from 1897 shows Company H from Manitowoc at its summer encampment at Camp Rahr in Clarks Mills. Company H would go on to fight in World War I in 1917 and receive a big send-off and welcome home parade in 1918. (Courtesy Manitowoc Public Library.)

This family photograph shows a father and his eight sons. The younger boys are all dressed in knickers. Many family photographs from that era were more formal and taken in a studio. It appears that two of the sons may be twins. (Courtesy Manitowoc Public Library.)

This would have been an unusual sight in 1905—an electric car being driven by a woman. Electric cars were somewhat of a status symbol. They were much more expensive than their gas-powered cousins. Many women preferred them because they were quieter and did not have the exhaust smell that came with gas-powered cars. Some of the better models could travel up to 15 miles per hour and go 100 miles on a single charge. (Courtesy Manitowoc Public Library.)

A group of men have gathered for a picnic and a baseball game at Wettencamp Flats in 1911. From left to right are (first row) Mike Auermiller, Al. Hoyer, Victor Klingholz, Emil Vollendorf, and Robert Heise; (second row) Emil Oberland, Chas Kulnick, John Meyer, Henry Meisner, Adam Hendrick, Alex Bahr, August Becker, Fred Carus, Frank Pitch, Alex Fischel, Herman Lenz, Anton Karnofsky, and A.J. Braxmeier; (third row) Ben Bean, Carl Hartwig, Joe Nemitz, Fred Lemke, Charles Schlei, Fred Schmidt, Christ Shade, Salty Bonk, John Kennedy, Aug. Mueller, Ed Goeters, and unidentified; (fourth row) Henry Schreihart, Al Shrimp Schroeder, John Kulnick, Ed Mueller, George Bean, Peter Broehl, John Mauser on horse, and Jim Kulnick on horse. (Courtesy Manitowoc Public Library.)

Passenger trains were an extremely popular mode of transportation in early Manitowoc County. Once the railroad came to the county, almost all the small towns were connected, and a trip to Manitowoc became much quicker and easier compared to traveling by horse and buggy. (Courtesy Manitowoc Public Library.)

An unidentified man and woman, dressed in their Sunday best, are getting ready to go for a ride in their horse-drawn buggy. The photograph was taken in an unidentified village in the county, but this scene would have been played out in any town on any given Sunday around 1900. (Courtesy Manitowoc Public Library.)

This photograph from July 1902 shows a picnic for the local Saengerbund club. A Saengerbund club was a group of Germans singers, usually but not always made up of just men. Once a year, they would get together and have a picnic. It is a safe bet that good German sausage and beer was consumed. (Courtesy Manitowoc Public Library.)

What might be happening in this photograph? This group of men is standing around a wagon. The second from the left is wearing a badge. Two beer cases can be seen on the front of the wagon. One is from the Rahr Brewery, and the other is from Schreihart. All the men look serious. (Courtesy Manitowoc Public Library.)

This was the first homestead of Friedrich and Wilhelmina Kluenker in America. The house was at the northwest corner of what is now Homestead and Wagon Wheel Roads. It is believed the man in the picture is Friedrich. They purchased the property in 1897 and built a log cabin. (Courtesy Manitowoc Public Library.)

This is Friedrich and Wilhelmina Kluenker's second house in America. It was built to the west of the original Kluenker home in 1909 for about $2,800 and included hardwood floors and oak trim. From left to right are Charles (29 years old), Sophie (32), Friedrich III, Wilhelmina "Minnie" (65), Friedrich II (67), and George (26). (Courtesy Manitowoc Public Library.)

Bibliography

Ertel, Barbara, ed. *Clearing the Land: Glimpses of Our Heritage*. 1976.

Manitowoc Herald Times.

Rappel, Joseph, ed. *A Centennial History of the Manitowoc County School*. 1948.

Vogel, Herbert, ed. *A Brief History of Valders*. 1986.

Consistent with our mission to preserve history on a local level, this book was printed in South Carolina on American-made paper and manufactured entirely in the United States. Products carrying the accredited Forest Stewardship Council (FSC) label are printed on 100 percent FSC-certified paper.